Whispers Of The Soul

A Journey Back to you

Akanksha Pokharna

BookLeaf
Publishing

India | USA | UK

Made with ❤ on the BookLeaf Publishing Platform
www.bookleafpub.in
www.bookleafpub.com

Dedication

To the ones who have felt lost, yet kept walking.
To the ones who have stumbled, yet found the strength
to rise.
To the ones who are still learning to love themselves—
piece by piece, day by day.
This book is for you.
For every heart that has known pain yet still beats with
hope,
for every soul that longs to be seen, to be heard, to be
understood—
may these words remind you of your light, your
strength, your infinite worth.
You are not lost—you are finding your way.
You are not behind—you are growing at your own
perfect pace.
You are not broken—you are becoming whole.
You are powerful. You are worthy. You are enough.
And the best is yet to come.
With love, light, and unwavering belief in you,
Akanksha

Preface

These words found me in quiet moments, in the pauses between breaths, in the stillness that life so often asks us to overlook. I cannot say I wrote them; rather, they flowed through me, like a gentle conversation with something deeper, something beyond.

This book is not about grand wisdom or perfect answers —it's simply a collection of reflections, feelings, and truths that surfaced when I slowed down enough to listen. If these words resonate with you, if they offer even a small sense of comfort or clarity, then perhaps they were always meant to reach you.

May you find yourself in these pages. May they remind you of the strength, love, and light that have been within you all along.

With warmth,

Akanksha

Acknowledgements

Some feelings are too big for words, but my heart tells me to try—because love, gratitude, and the people who stand by us deserve to be spoken about.

Aditya, you are my heart's greatest comfort. With you, I feel home—in the quiet moments, in the laughter, in the way you understand me without me having to explain. You have held me through my strongest and weakest days, through my doubts and dreams. Thank you for being my rock, my love, my safe place. I wouldn't be me without you.

Arisht and Arah, my beautiful children, you are my reason, my joy, my everything. Your love is the purest thing I have ever known. You remind me every day to live fully, love deeply, and find wonder in the little things. Being your mother is the greatest blessing of my life.

To our parents, thank you for your endless love, for your prayers, for being our foundation. Every lesson, every sacrifice, every word of encouragement has shaped me. We are who we are because of you.

To my family, your love has been a constant presence, lifting me up in ways you may not even realize. Your support, your laughter, your kindness—they mean more to me than I can ever express.

And to **you**, the one holding this book—thank you for being a part of this journey. This book carries a piece of my heart, and if even one word in these pages speaks to you, then it has found its purpose.

With love and gratitude,
Akanksha

1. Being Me

There was a time I tried to be
like the world around me—
speaking their words, following their ways,
hoping to feel like I belonged.
I silenced my heart, dimmed my light,
tried to fit into spaces never meant for me.
But the more I tried, the more I felt lost.

Life has a way of bringing you home.
Through love, through loss, through quiet whispers,
it reminded me—
I was never meant to be like them. I was meant to be me.

Not perfect, not someone else,
just real, just true.
And that is enough.

2. Home Within

For a long time, I looked outside—
for answers, for direction, for a sign.
I thought the world would show me the way,
so I followed, listened, and tried to stay.

I chased the noise, ran with the crowd,
thinking that's what life's about.
But the more I searched, the more I knew,
the path was always leading me *through*.

Not out there, not far away,
but deep within, clear as day.
In the quiet, in my own space,
I found my home, my truth, my place.

3. Trust Youself

You don't have to have it all figured out.
You don't need every answer today.
Life unfolds in its own time,
revealing what you're ready to see.

The world may tell you to doubt,
to second-guess, to seek approval.
But deep inside, there is a knowing—
a quiet, steady voice that never wavers.
Close your eyes. Breathe. Listen.
You are stronger than you think,
wiser than you know,
and exactly where you need to be.
Trust yourself.
You already hold the answers within.

4. The Strength to Begin Again

There comes a moment
when you decide
not to be held by the past,
not to fear the unknown,
but to step forward with strength.
Letting go isn't easy,
but staying the same isn't either.
The past may whisper reasons to stay,
but I have outgrown its echo.
Deep inside, I know
I am not meant to stay where I was.
I am meant to rise,
to trust,
to step into what's next.
So I take the first step,
not because I have all the answers,
but because I refuse to stand still.
Every ending is also a beginning.
And I am ready

not just to walk away,
but to walk toward something greater.

5

5. Unlearning

I used to think I had to become more—
do more, prove more, be more.
But life, in its gentle way,
showed me the truth.
It was never about adding,
but about letting go.
Letting go of the need to explain myself,
the weight of expectations,
the voices that told me who I should be.
With every unlearning, I feel lighter.
Not because I have less,
but because I am finally free.
I am not lost.
I am not becoming.
I am simply returning—
to the person I was always meant to be.

6. Quiet Strength

I used to think strength
meant standing tall,
never breaking,
never losing my way.
But life, in its quiet wisdom,
showed me the truth.
Strength is not in the noise,
not in the battles won,
not in proving anything to anyone.
It is in the silent wars we fight within,
the nights we sit with our pain
and still choose to believe in tomorrow.
It is in the breaking and the mending,
the falling and the rising,
the soft whisper inside that says—
"You are not done yet."
True strength isn't in never falling,
but in the courage to rise,
again and again,
with an open heart.

7. Reflection

I used to move so fast,
always reaching for the next thing,
always chasing what's ahead.
I never stopped long enough
to see how far I had come,
to listen to the quiet wisdom within.
But when I finally paused,
I saw the journey differently—
not as a race to win,
but as a path to understand.
Every step, even the missteps,
had shaped me.
Every detour had something to teach.
Reflection is not about looking back with regret,
but with gratitude—
for the lessons,
for the growth,
for the person I have become.

8. Growing Through It

I used to wonder why some days felt heavier than others,
why life didn't always go as planned, why the hard
moments came uninvited.
But with time, I learned— growth doesn't happen in ease
alone. It happens in the struggles, in the quiet strength
we find when things don't go our way.
Every challenge shaped me, every setback taught me,
every tear watered something new within me.
I am not who I was before— not because life was always
kind, but because I found a way to grow, even through
the storms.

9. Loving the Person You Are Today

I spent so long
waiting to feel worthy,
measuring myself
against expectations
I never chose.

For every step forward,
I saw a hundred reasons
I wasn't enough.
But one day, I looked closer—
not at what was missing,
but at what had always been there.
Strength in my scars,
wisdom in my wounds,
beauty in simply being.
So now, I stand with myself,
not against.
I embrace the person I am,
not the one I thought I had to be.

And in that quiet acceptance,
I find something I searched for all along—
peace.

10. Strength in Softness

We're often told to protect our hearts,
to guard against pain and disappointment.
But I've come to realize—
there's power in staying open.
It's not about being tough all the time.
It's about being gentle with ourselves,
allowing ourselves to feel,
and trusting that we can handle whatever   comes.
True strength isn't in building walls
to keep out the hurt,
but in the courage to stay soft,
even when it feels uncertain.
We don't need to be unbreakable.
Sometimes, it's in our softness,
our vulnerability,
that we find the deepest strength.
Because the more we open up,
the more we learn how to hold ourselves—
gently, lovingly, and with grace.

11. Flow with Time

Sometimes, life feels like a river,
rushing fast, pulling me along,
and I try to hold on tight,
thinking I can control it all.
But I've learned that time
has its own rhythm,
and all I can do
is flow with it, gently.
The moments pass,
and with each one,
I grow a little more.
I don't need to fight it—
I just need to trust.
So I let go,
and let time carry me,
knowing wherever it leads,
I will be okay.

12. Embracing the Struggle

We all think there's a way to get it right—
a path where mistakes are not allowed,
where everything falls into place
and we move through life effortlessly.
But life doesn't follow that script.
It's not about perfection.
It's about being real,
with all the bumps, the cracks, the scars.
We all stumble, we all fall,
wondering if we'll ever find our way.
But in those moments,
we find something deep
strength in standing back up,
even when we don't have the answers.
The beauty isn't in the perfect journey,
but in the grace we find in the struggle.
It's in learning to love ourselves,
even when we're broken,
and realizing that the path itself
is what shapes us.

We're all still growing.
And that's more than enough.

15

13. True Success

Success isn't about the things we collect,
or the titles we wear.
It's not in the noise or the praise.
Success is in the quiet moments—
when we can lay down at night
and feel peace in our hearts,
knowing we gave our best,
even when everything didn't go as planned.

It's in the simple things—
showing up when life gets tough,
being there for the ones we love,
even when we feel worn out.
Success is in choosing kindness,
even when it's hard,
and learning to forgive,
not just others, but ourselves too.

At the end of the day,
success is the calm we feel in our soul,

knowing we were true to ourselves,
that we loved deeply,
and that, despite everything,
we were enough.

14. Self Love

We often give and give,
until we feel we have nothing left to offer.
We try to love others,
to hold them,
to care for them,
but forget to hold ourselves first.
How can you offer light
when your own flame is flickering?
How can you lift others
when your own strength is weak?
You can't pour from an empty jar.
Self-love isn't just a luxury;
it's the foundation.
Without it, every act of love becomes a sacrifice,
draining you bit by bit.
But when you fill your heart,
when you nurture your soul,
you begin to overflow.
Your love doesn't deplete you;
it multiplies,

it strengthens,
it sustains.
So take a moment—
pause, breathe, refill.
Be gentle with yourself.
And know that when you fill your own jar,
you have more than enough to give.
Only then can you truly pour out love
without fear of running dry.

15. A Shift in View

Sometimes we get lost in how we see things,
Stuck in the same thoughts, the same way of feeling.
But what if we could pause, just for a moment,
And look at it all from a different place?
What if we saw the good in the bad,
The lessons hidden in the hurt?
What if we stopped wondering "Why me?"
And started asking, "What will I learn?"
A new way of looking doesn't change what's true,
But it makes it easier to get through.
It doesn't take away the struggle,
But helps us find strength where we thought we had
none.
When life feels heavy, and we feel small,
A shift in how we see it can change it all.
Sometimes, a new perspective is all we need,
To see the beauty and let our hearts breathe.

16. Embrace the Unknown

You know, we all get so comfortable with what we know,
the paths we've walked a hundred times,
the places that feel safe and familiar.
But sometimes, life softly whispers,
asking us to let go,
to take a step into something different.
I know, it's scary.
The future isn't clear, and it's easy to be afraid.
But that uncertainty, that unknown,
it holds something powerful.
A strength we don't always see,
but it's there, waiting for us to find it.
We don't have to have everything figured out,
or know exactly where we're going.
Sometimes, the magic is in just trusting,
in letting life unfold,
and allowing ourselves to be part of the journey.
The unknown isn't something to fear,
it's actually where we grow,
where we discover parts of ourselves

we never knew existed.
It's the place where we become stronger,
braver, more alive.
So, let's embrace the unknown, together.
With open hearts, with trust.
Because in that space, something beautiful happens—
we find ourselves.

17. We Are All Connected

When we look for the good in others,
we start to see it in ourselves too.
A smile, a kind word, a gentle hand—
these little things remind us of the love inside.
When we lift someone up,
we feel lifted too.
Their joy becomes ours,
and our hearts feel lighter.
We're all connected,
in ways we often can't see,
but when we search for the best in others,
we end up finding it in ourselves.
Love, kindness, joy—
they flow back and forth,
making life a little brighter,
a little more beautiful.

18. The Unseen Path

It may feel like you're standing still,
Like time is slipping through your hands.
But beneath the surface, change is happening,
In ways you can't see or understand.

Like the seed buried deep in the earth,
Quietly growing, unseen by the eye.
It doesn't rush, doesn't force its bloom,
But in time, it will reach for the sky.
Or like the night before the dawn,
When darkness seems to have no end.
But in that stillness, the light is waiting,
Ready to rise, ready to ascend.

Every step you take, no matter how small,
Is part of a story you're writing.
Even in the moments of stillness,
The path ahead is quietly unfolding.
So trust in the process, trust in the time,
For what's meant for you will come.

Like the seed, like the night,
You're growing into what you've always been.

25

19. The Value of a Moment

We don't always see the beauty
In the moments that slip by,
We're lost in what's next, in the rush,
Not knowing how time passes by.
A smile, a hug, just being together,
We think they're small, but they're not.
They're the heartbeat of life, softly present,
The love that fills the empty spots.
It's only when they're gone,
When the moment has passed,
That we realize how precious it was,
How we should've made it last.
So hold each moment close, my friend,
Because the now won't stay forever.
The laughter, the love, the quiet peace—
Those are the moments we'll remember.
When we look back, we'll see the truth—
The simple things meant the most.
The ones we almost let slip away,
Were the ones we loved the most.

20. Letting Yourself Be Seen

There's a quiet kind of strength
in allowing yourself to be seen—
in standing in your truth,
bare and unguarded.
We all have places we hide,
parts of us we think are too much,
too broken,
too raw.
But when we let them show,
we discover that these parts
are not flaws,
but the very things that make us whole.
To be seen is to trust,
to trust that we are enough
just as we are,
and that the world will meet us with love
and understanding,

not judgment.
It's not about being perfect.
It's about being real.
And in that realness,
we find connection,
we find healing,
we find ourselves.
Let yourself be seen,
not to be admired,
but to remind yourself
that you are worthy of being loved—
just as you are.

21. Healing takes time

Healing isn't a straight path.
It's not a race or a deadline.
Some days, you'll feel light and whole.
Other days, the weight will return,
and that's okay.
Scars don't mean you're broken.
They mean you survived.
Pain doesn't mean you're failing.
It means you're feeling.
Let yourself rest.
Let yourself breathe.
Let yourself take the time you need.
Healing doesn't mean going back
to who you were before.
It means becoming who you were meant to be
all along.

22. Even on the Hard Days

On the days when you feel like you're failing,
when nothing seems to go right,
when the voice in your head is unkind—
pause, take a breath, and remember this:
You are not meant to be perfect.
You are meant to be real.
Real means messy.
Real means growing.
Real means showing up, even when it's hard.
Love yourself through it all.
Not just when you're shining,
but when you're stumbling, too.
Not just when you feel strong,
but when all you can do is get through the day.
You are not failing.
You are learning.
You are healing.
You are growing.
And through it all,

you are worthy of love—
especially from yourself.

23. Divine Presence

You call out for me,
wondering if I hear you,
if I understand your pain,
if I see the weight you carry.
My child, I have never left.
I was there in your quiet moments,
when you felt unseen,
when your heart ached in silence,
when you thought you walked alone.
I was the strength in your steps,
the breath that kept you going,
the gentle whisper that said,
"Trust, keep moving, you are loved."

You search for me in the stars,
in signs, in miracles,
but I have always been closer than that—
woven into your laughter,
cradled in your tears,
beating softly within your heart.

I was there when you stumbled,
and I was there when you rose,
through every storm,
through every dark night,
I held you in my arms,
even when you forgot,
even when you doubted,
even when you thought you had lost me.
You have never been alone.
Not for a single breath.
I have always been here,
a divine presence, steady and pure,
watching over you with love,
and I always will be.

24. The Art of Embracing Dislike

You must learn the art of being disliked,
To free yourself from the weight of others' eyes.
For not everyone will understand your heart,
And that's okay, it's where freedom starts.

You see, opinions will come, as they always do,
But their voices are not the ones to define you.
The world will judge, will try to sway,
But your worth is found in your own way.

You may find yourself standing alone,
As you walk a path that's all your own.
But in that solitude, you will find peace,
A quiet strength, a sense of release.
To be disliked is not a defeat,
But a chance to stand tall on your own two feet.
For when you let go of others' views,
You make room for your own truth to bloom.
So let them speak, let them turn away,

For your freedom lies in being true every day.
The opinions of others are fleeting, after all,
But your true self, it will never fall.

25. It's Okay to Cry

They say men shouldn't cry,
that strength means silence,
that holding it in
makes you brave.

But I have seen the bravest hearts
break open with tears,
felt the deepest love
spill through quiet sobs.
Tears don't make us weak—
they make us real.
They hold the words
we cannot say,
the love we cannot measure,
the pain we finally set free.

Hearts that feel will sometimes weep,
just like the sky lets go of the rain—
and after the storm,
the earth breathes again,

soft, fresh, alive.

So let your heart be light,
let your soul be free.
Tears are not shameful,
they are sacred—
a sign that we have loved,
that we have felt,
that we are human.

26. A Love That Stays

I once thought love was in the grand gestures,
in perfect words spoken at the perfect time,
in promises so strong they could never break.
But love—real love—
is quieter than that.
It's in the way you stood beside me,
not to carry my pain,
but to remind me I didn't have to carry it alone.

It's in the way you never looked away,
even when I was tired,
even when I was afraid,
even when I was not the strongest version of myself.

You never tried to change me,
never asked me to be less,
never made me feel like a burden.
You simply stayed.
Through the fear, through the silence,
through the days that stretched too long—

you stayed.
You never rushed me to heal,
never filled the quiet with empty words.
You just held space,
held my hand,
held me in ways deeper than language.

Love like this doesn't need to be loud.
It doesn't ask for proof.
It simply stays—
steady, certain, unshaken.

And for that, for you,
I am forever grateful.

27. The Choice Is Yours

Life will always have its ups and downs,
its joys and sorrows, its light and shadow.
You may not control everything that happens,
but you can choose how you meet it.
The same mornings, the same challenges—
but now, you rise with purpose.
The same people, the same past—
but now, you see them with love and understanding, not
pain.
Nothing outside has changed overnight,
but inside—you have.
You've made space for peace, for joy, for something
lighter.
You've chosen to grow instead of staying stuck.
And suddenly, life feels different.
The struggles become lessons.
The setbacks become stepping stones.
The same people who once tested you become a blessing.
Every day is a new beginning.
Every moment holds a choice.

To see light, to embrace love, to move forward with
hope.
And with every breath,
you get to choose joy.

28. Unapologetically You

You are not here to be perfect.
You are here to be real.
To laugh until your stomach hurts,
to cry when your heart feels heavy,
to love without holding back.
Some will understand you, some won't—
but that's okay.
The ones who truly see you will stay,
and their love will feel like home.
So don't shrink yourself to fit.
Don't quiet your dreams to please.
You are meant to live fully,
to take up space, to shine in your own way.

Be kind. Be bold. Be you.
And never apologize for the heart that makes you who
you are.

29. Be Someone's Hope

Sit with them.
Not to fix, not to fill the silence,
just to be there.
Sometimes, that's all we need—
to know someone cares enough to stay.
Hold their hand when words won't come.
Not to pull them out of their pain,
but to remind them they're still here,
they still matter,
even when they feel like they don't.
Stay, even when they turn away.
Not to force yourself in,
but to show them that love—real love—
doesn't leave when things get hard.
I know this because I've been there too.
I've felt the kind of pain
that makes you wonder
if anyone would notice if you disappeared.
And then—
hands reached for me,

soft voices whispered,
"You don't have to go through this alone."
Maybe that's why I believe in staying now.
Because I know what it's like
to be held when I thought I would fall.
To be seen when I felt invisible.
To be loved when I didn't feel worthy of love.
Hope isn't some grand gesture.
It's small, quiet, steady.
A presence that doesn't fade.
A love that doesn't walk away.
A light in the dark that says—
"I see you. I'm here. And I won't let go."

30. Your Story is Still Being Written

Your story isn't over yet.
I know some chapters have been hard,
some pages filled with tears,
some nights heavier than words.
But you're still here.
And that means something.
The past may have shaped you,
but it does not hold the pen.
You do.
With every breath, every step,
you are writing something new.
Not every path has been clear,
not every dream has stayed the same.
But growth isn't always loud—
sometimes, it's just the quiet strength
to keep going.
So take a deep breath, my friend.
Turn the page. Trust the unfolding.

Your story is still being written—
and the best parts are yet to come.

31. Rest is Revolutionary

In a world that never slows down,
where rest feels like falling behind,
I want you to remember, love—
you are not here to race through life.
You were never meant to run on empty,
to prove your worth in exhaustion,
to keep going when your heart is asking you to pause.
So take a breath.
Soften.
Let yourself rest, not because everything is done,
but because *you* deserve care too.
Rest is not a weakness.
It is love—
a gentle way of saying, *I matter too.*
The world will keep moving,
but, my love, you are allowed to slow down,
to breathe,
to simply *be.*

32. Becoming Your Own Safe Place

There will be days
when no one has the right words,
when the comfort you seek
does not arrive,
when even the ones who love you
cannot quite reach where it hurts.
And in those moments, love,
you may wonder—
who will hold you?
Who will understand?
But listen closely.
Beneath the noise, beneath the ache,
there is a quiet voice within you,
steady, unwavering, true.
Sit with yourself.
Wrap your own arms around your heart.
Let your breath remind you—
you have always been here for you.
Not every wound needs fixing.

Not every sorrow needs a cure.
Sometimes, you just need space
to feel, to rest, to be.
And that is enough.
You are enough.
You are your own safe place,
not because life is easy,
but because you have learned
to be gentle with yourself.
And that, my love,
is the deepest kind of love there is.

33. A Blessing You Can't See Yet

I know it doesn't feel like it now,
but one day, you'll look back and understand.
The closed door.
The unexpected turn.
The loss that felt too heavy to carry.
You thought it was breaking you,
but it was guiding you.
Life has a way of protecting us
in ways we don't recognize at first.
Sometimes, what feels like an ending
is just love rerouting you to something better.
So hold on, love.
One day, you'll see—
this was a blessing in disguise all along.

34. The Dance of Light and Shadow

Life is both—
the warmth of the sun,
the hush of the night,
the joy of laughter,
the weight of tears.
You cannot have one without the other.
The moon needs darkness to shine,
the river needs rocks to sing,
and you, my love,
need both sorrow and joy
to truly feel alive.
Do not fear the pain—
it is shaping you.
Do not cling to the joy—
it is teaching you.
Let life hold you in its rhythm,
rising, falling, breaking, healing.
For even in your darkest hour,
the light has not left you.

It is here,
waiting for you to see.

52

35. The Joy of Missing Out

There is peace in the quiet,
in the nights without noise,
in choosing slow moments
over a world that rushes by.
No need to be everywhere,
no need to be seen—
joy is not in the crowd,
but in the stillness between.
A book half-read, a walk alone,
a cup of tea with no rush.
The freedom to breathe,
to just be, without needing more.
Let the world chase,
let it hurry and call—
there is joy in missing out,
in knowing you have enough.

36. Now Is All We Have

Not yesterday's regrets,
not tomorrow's worries—
just this moment, right here, right now.
A warm cup of tea in your hands,
shared with someone you love,
soft conversations, unhurried and real,
laughter filling the quiet spaces,
the comfort of simply being together—
life is happening in these small, ordinary moments.
We keep waiting—
for the perfect time,
for everything to make sense,
for some future where we'll finally feel at peace.
But love, what if that moment is this one?
What if joy isn't something we chase,
but something we notice?
Breathe.
Feel.
Be here.
Now is all we have.

And right now—
is enough.

37. Held by Grace

There was a time I felt lost,
like the ground beneath me had disappeared.
My body was tired, my heart was heavy,
and I wondered if I would ever feel whole again.
In the quiet of my pain, I whispered, *Why, God?*
And though no voice thundered from the sky,
I felt something—soft but certain,
a presence that wrapped around me like a warm
embrace.
God didn't take away my struggles,
but He walked beside me through them.
In the hands that held mine,
in the voices that reminded me to keep going,
in the love that never left, even on my hardest days.
He showed me His presence
in the warmth of my child's hug,
in the quiet strength of my love,
who stood like an unshaken tree in my storm,
holding me up when I felt I could no longer stand,
in the laughter of my family that filled the empty spaces,

in the unwavering love of my friends,
and in the kindness of strangers who became angels in
disguise.
I thought I was breaking,
but He was rebuilding me.
Not back to who I was,
but into someone even stronger, even wiser
someone who knows that no matter how dark the night,
morning always comes.

38. Roots and Wings

I stand with my feet in the earth,
Feeling the love that's always here,
The strength that lifts me when I fall,
A gentle light that's always near.
The sky calls, and my heart wants to fly,
To chase my dreams, to reach the sky.
But as I stretch towards something new,
I remember where I started, and who I grew into.
My roots are deep, my wings are wide,
They help me move with every stride.
The love that holds me, the dreams I chase,
Together, they guide me in every space.
I am both grounded and free,
Learning to rise, but still holding on to me.
Every step, every breath, I know,
That love will always help me grow.
I fly with hope, I soar with grace,
And in my roots, I find my place.
No matter where my wings may roam,
My heart will always know its home.

39. The Change Begins with You

I spent so long searching—
for happiness, for love, for peace.
I thought the world had to change,
that people had to be kinder,
that life should be easier,
that things had to be fairer.
But life doesn't work that way, does it?
One day, tired from the chase,
I stopped and sat quietly.
No distractions, no running—
just me, my breath, my heart.
And in that quiet, a thought came—
"What if the change begins with you?"
Not the world, not others, not tomorrow.
Just you.
The way you see,
the way you feel,
the love you give yourself.
So I let go.

I stopped waiting for others to complete me.
I started giving love to myself,
because we can't pour love from an empty cup.
And something simple happened—
Life didn't need to be perfect,
but I found peace.
Things didn't always go my way,
but I learned to go with the flow.
I changed,
and life changed with me.
And maybe—just maybe—
that was the secret all along.

40. When We Give Freely

I've learned that when we give freely,
without holding anything back,
there's always more to share—
love, kindness, hope—
they never run out.
It begins with the smallest gestures—
a smile, a kind word,
a hand to lift someone up.
These acts come from a place of love,
simply because they feel true.
And here's what I've discovered—
the more I give,
the more life gives back.
Not always in ways I expect,
but in ways that touch my soul.
For every kind word,
something sweeter returns.
For every hand extended,
the world offers something back to me.
Life doesn't take from me,

it multiplies what I give.
In the quiet moments,
peace, joy, love
they find their way back to me,
coming back in ways I never imagined.
So I give, with love, with no fear,
and trust that what I put into the world
will always return to me—
multiplied.

41. The Purpose of My Life

I used to wonder,
Why am I here?
What is mine to do,
to give,
to become?
I searched for answers in the world,
in titles, in achievements,
in the expectations of others.
But the more I searched outside,
the more lost I felt within.
Then one day, in the quiet,
I heard the truth—
My purpose was never a destination,
never a single grand moment.
It was in the way I love,
the way I show up,
the way I keep going,
even when it's hard.
My purpose is not to be perfect,
but to be real.

To live with an open heart,
to grow, to heal,
to give what I can,
and to trust that is enough.
Maybe that's what purpose really is—
not something to find,
but something to *live*,
every single day.

42. Too Late to See

Life is simple, we make it hard,
Chasing dreams, always on guard.
We run so fast, we miss the light,
The quiet moments that feel right.
We think we need more than we've got,
Striving for something we've already sought.
The truth is gentle, soft, and near,
But we're too busy to let it appear.
We only see it when it's too late,
When we realize the simple fate.
That life is here, in every breath,
In every pause, in every step.
And though we've learned when time has flown,
We finally see we're not alone.
The beauty's always been around,
In the stillness, peace is found.

43. Through Every Storm, With You

We've seen the highs,
and we've weathered the lows,
our hearts dancing through moments,
both calm and wild.
Together, we've grown—
not just in time,
but in love,
in understanding,
in patience,
in the quiet ways we've learned to hold each
other.
Through every challenge,
we've found strength in each other's arms,
and in every joy,
we've doubled the happiness we've shared.
I love my life with you,

with all its imperfections,
its twists and turns,
its messes and miracles.
You are my constant,
the steady hand I reach for in the dark,
the warmth in my coldest moments,
the laughter in my hardest days.
Together, we have built something beautiful—
a love that doesn't shy away from the storms,
but stands strong,
side by side,
with roots deep enough to hold us,
even when the winds blow fierce.
I love my life with you,
and in your eyes, I see all the reasons I'm home.

44. The Art of Letting Go

I started with my home—
old clothes, forgotten papers,
things I held onto "just in case."
I let them go, one by one,
and suddenly, my space could breathe again.
But then I noticed—
the real clutter wasn't just on the shelves.
It was in my mind, in my heart.
Old regrets, unspoken worries,
memories I replayed too often,
pain I thought I had to carry.
So, I let go again.
The guilt that wasn't mine to hold.
The need to be perfect.
The weight of trying to be everything to everyone.
And then—
I forgave.
Myself, for not knowing better before.
Others, for the things they never even realized.
I set them free.

I set *myself* free.
And in that space, something beautiful happened—
I felt lighter, clearer,
as if my soul had room to stretch,
as if I had finally made space for *me.*
Because life isn't about holding onto everything.
It's about choosing what truly matters,
forgiving what once weighed you down,
and letting the rest go.

45. A Letter to My Younger Self

Dear Younger Me,

I see you there, with dreams so quiet,

Fears unspoken, yet a heart so bright.

Wide open to the world, unsure of your place,

Wishing I could reach through time, give you grace.

You are enough, just as you are,

You always have been, like a distant star.

I know you think you have to stand strong,

Carrying it all, but you don't have to for long.

Let people in, let them see the real you,

The right ones will stay, the others will drift through.

Don't worry about the unknown, the things you can't

see,

Most of it will pass or shape you, and you'll be free.

You'll lose things, and yes, it will hurt,

But in the loss, you'll find love, peace, and your worth.

Grief and joy, together they'll dance,

And life isn't about the end, but this very chance.

So breathe, my love, slow down, and be still,

Trust yourself, follow your heart's gentle will.
Keep your heart open, through every trial,
Life will carry you, just take it mile by mile.
With love,
Me

46. You Are Perfect as You Are

In the quiet of your being, there's a truth untold,
You are perfect as you are, with a heart both brave and bold.
No need to wear a mask, no need to change your face,
You are a universe, existing in its perfect place.
The weight you carry, the stories you've known,
They don't define you; they've helped you grow.
Every scar, every tear that's fallen free,
Has shaped the beauty of your soul, for all to see.
There is no need to rush, no need to chase,
For time is not your enemy, it is your grace.
In every breath, in every moment you hold dear,
You are enough, my love, you've always been here.
Your worth is not measured by what you do or achieve,
But by the love you give and the peace you believe.
You are the quiet strength that rises from within,
A sacred whisper, where your journey begins.
So be still for a moment, and just let it be,
You are perfect, simply by being free.

No change is needed, no fault to mend,
You are enough, my dear, from beginning to end.

73

47. Whispers of Gratitude

I wake—not just to another day,
but to a body that still carries me,
to a heart that still beats,
to a life that is still unfolding.
Thank you, sky—not just for the sunshine,
but for the storms that have tested me,
for the winds that have pushed me forward
when I was too afraid to move.
Thank you, earth—not just for steady ground,
but for the falls that taught me how to rise,
for the seasons that remind me
nothing stays the same, and that's okay.
Thank you, pain—not just for the lessons,
but for slowing me down, for making me feel,
for breaking me open when I tried so hard to stay whole.
For reminding me that healing is not about going back—
but about becoming something new.
Thank you, love—not just for the moments that felt easy,
but for the ones that stretched me, unraveled me,
taught me that love is not just in the words,

but in the silence, the presence, the understanding.
Thank you, life—not just for the picture-perfect
moments,
but for the ones I didn't ask for,
the detours that led me where I needed to go,
the hands that held me when I couldn't hold myself.
For every breath, every lesson, every chance to begin
again.
For it all.
For it all.

48. Freedom

Freedom is not just running wild,
not the wind calling like a child.
It's the space to breathe, to be,
to live this life wholeheartedly.
It's not about breaking away,
but finding peace in where I stay.
Not about silence, not about sound,
but feeling safe in what I've found.
Freedom is love without a chain,
a heart that sings beyond the pain.
It's choosing joy, it's letting go,
trusting life will always flow.
Not in the sky, not in the sea,
freedom is right here in me.

49. Faith and Fear

Fear shows up uninvited.
It sits next to me and says,
"What if you fail? What if you're not enough?"
It makes my heart race, my hands cold.
It makes me overthink, hesitate, shrink.

But faith...
Faith doesn't push its way in.
It waits, gentle, steady, patient.
It doesn't fight fear—it just sits beside it and says,
"You don't have to see the whole path. Just take one
step."

Fear wants control, certainty, guarantees.
Faith asks for trust, surrender, a deep breath.
Fear shouts, "What if everything falls apart?"
Faith whispers, "What if everything falls into place?"

Some days, fear is louder.
Some days, faith feels far away.

But I remind myself—
Fear is a story.
Faith is a choice.

And when I don't know what to do,
I close my eyes, put my hand on my heart,
and take one small step—toward faith.

50. Bucket List

I don't want a list of things to check off,
rushing from one dream to the next.
I just want to live—really live.
I want to wake up with gratitude,
feel the morning sun on my face,
drink my tea slowly,
and breathe without hurry.
I want to laugh until I can't breathe,
hug a little longer,
say "I love you" without holding back,
and mean it every time.
I want to sit with the people I love,
with no phones, no distractions—
just stories, just presence, just us.
I want to walk barefoot on the grass,
watch the sky change colors,
get lost in deep conversations,
and never be too busy to notice life happening.
Because in the end,
it won't matter how far I traveled

or how many things I achieved.
What will matter is how deeply I lived,
how much love I gave,
and how many moments I truly felt.

51. God Sent You for Me

I love my life with you—
not because it's perfect,
but because with you, even the imperfections feel
beautiful.
You are my calm in the chaos,
my laughter on the hard days,
the warmth I never knew my soul needed.
I look at you and feel in my heart—
God must have sent you just for me.
Not to complete me,
but to walk this journey beside me,
to remind me what love truly feels like.
With you, home is not a place,
it's a feeling.
And every single day,
I thank the universe for you.

52. A Love Letter to Life

Dear Life,

You have been both gentle and wild,

a soft breeze and a raging storm.

You have knocked me down,

but you have also lifted me higher than I ever dreamed.

You have taken from me,

but given me even more.

You have tested my strength,

only to show me I was unbreakable.

You have taught me that love is not just in the grand

moments,

but in the quiet ones—

in morning sunlight on my face,

in laughter that echoes long after it's gone,

in the warmth of a hand holding mine.

I have cried for you,

ached for you,

but oh, how I have loved you.

And through it all,

you have whispered back,

reminding me—
I was always meant to be here,
to feel, to grow, to love,
to live.
And so, I will.
With all my heart.
With all my soul.
For as long as you will have me.
With love,
Me

53. Death

I used to fear you—
the silence, the ending, the unknown.
But now, I see you differently.
Not as darkness,
but as a doorway.
You are not the thief I once thought you were.
You don't take,
you return.
Back to the stars, back to the earth,
back to the love we were made from.
You are not cold, not cruel—
just a whisper, calling us home.
And when my time comes,
I will not run.
I will walk toward you,
with a heart full of life,
knowing I have lived,
knowing I have loved,
knowing I was never meant to stay.
And in that final breath,

I will not say goodbye—
only, *I'll see you again.*

85

54. The Gift of Difficult People

Not everyone who crosses our path is easy to love.
Some test our patience, push us beyond what feels
comfortable,
and make us wonder about the goodness we try to hold
on to.
But maybe—just maybe—
they come into our lives for a reason.
Maybe they aren't roadblocks,
but lessons in human form.
Perhaps they are mirrors,
reflecting the parts of ourselves we need to heal.
The ones who challenge us
show us the power of patience.
The ones who misunderstand us
help us find clarity.
The ones who hurt us
teach us the strength we didn't know we had.
They're not here to break us,
but to shape us.

To stretch our hearts,
and remind us who we are,
and who we never want to become.
So, instead of asking, Why them?
maybe the better question is, What are they here to teach
me?
And then, with an open heart,
we take the lesson,
let go of the bitterness,
and grow.

55. Imperfectly Me

Imperfectly me, and that's just fine,
I don't need to be flawless to let myself shine.
Some days I'm steady, some days I fall,
But I keep going—that's enough after all.

I carry scars, I carry grace,
Lessons etched in time and place.
Each crack, a space where light breaks through,
Each mistake, a step that helped me grow too.
I don't run after perfection now,
I live in the moment, here and now.
Every flaw, a part of my story,
Every wound, a lesson in love and glory.

So here I stand, just as I am,
Not perfect, not broken—just whole in my hands.
With an open heart, with roots held deep,
Imperfectly me—and at peace with it.

56. Grateful for Every Soul

If today were my last, and I looked back on my life,
I wouldn't count the days or measure the years.
I would remember the souls who touched my heart,
For they were the true gifts of this journey.
Some came like soft whispers, bringing love,
Their presence a warm embrace on weary days.
Some came as storms, shaking my ground,
Yet even in the thunder, there was wisdom.
The ones who stayed became my home,
Their love, a place where I could rest.
The ones who left taught me to trust,
That even endings have their own kind of grace.
I carry no bitterness, no weight, only love,
For every soul, in joy or in pain,
Was sent to shape me, to teach me, to awaken me.
And when my time comes, I will close my eyes,
With a heart full, a soul light,
Grateful for every hello, every goodbye,
And for the love that lived in between.

57. Trust the Divine

Not everything will make sense.
Not every door will open when you knock.
Some paths will twist and turn,
leading you where you never planned to go.
But trust—
there is a rhythm,
a wisdom far greater than yours,
guiding you,
even when you cannot see.
The delays, the detours,
the unanswered prayers—
they are not rejections,
but redirections.
You are being held,
you are being led.
So breathe,
let go of the need to control,
and trust—
the Divine knows the way.

58. Manifest

Close your eyes.
Feel it.
The life you dream of,
the love you long for,
the peace you seek—
it already exists within you.
You are not waiting for it to arrive.
You are growing into the person
who can receive it.
Every thought, every step,
every moment of trust
is shaping the path ahead.
Let go of doubt,
let go of fear.
Speak as if it's already yours.
Walk as if the universe
is moving with you.
Because it is.

59. Be Weird

Be weird.
Be the one who laughs too loud,
who dances without a reason,
who dreams with eyes wide open.
Be the one who feels everything—
who cries at beauty,
who sees magic in the smallest moments,
who believes in things no one else does.
Let them call you different.
Let them not understand.
You weren't meant to fit in;
you were meant to be free.
You were made to run wild,
to love without fear,
to color outside the lines of this world.
So be weird. Be real. Be you.
Because the world doesn't need more of the same.
It needs more hearts unafraid to shine.

60. Morning with God

Before the world demands anything of me,
before the noise and the lists and the rush—
I sit in the quiet, just breathing, just being.
I don't come with perfect prayers,
I don't try to impress Him with my words.
I just show up—tired, hopeful, messy, real.
And somehow, that's enough.
Because He's never asked me to be more,
never needed me to have it all together.
He just wants me as I am.
So I sit, let the morning hold me,
let the silence speak what words cannot.
And in the stillness, I know—
I am seen, I am safe, I am loved.

61. Build or Blame

You can build a better tomorrow,
or you can sit in the ruins of yesterday,
pointing fingers at the past,
waiting for it to change.
You can hold onto what broke you,
let it define you,
or you can rise from it,
let it shape you into something stronger.
Blame is easy.
It asks nothing of you but to stay the same.
Growth is harder.
It calls you forward,
asks you to step into the unknown,
to believe in something better.
The choice is always yours—
stay stuck in the story that hurt you,
or write a new one,
one where you are not just a survivor,
but a creator of your own life.

62. One Day You Realize

One day, you realize
you don't have enough time—
not for everything you've dreamed of,
not for all the things you've wanted to do.
The days slip by,
quiet as they pass,
until you wake up
and feel the weight of moments missed.
The dreams that were left behind,
the calls you didn't make,
the quiet joys you didn't savor.
But in that realization,
there's something beautiful too—
a soft, gentle reminder
that time is precious,
that every second matters
more than we sometimes think.
And so, you start—
not with regret,
but with a promise to yourself,

to not wait for perfect moments,
but to make each moment count.
You begin to love deeper,
to speak your truth louder,
to hold the things that matter close,
and let go of the noise
that once filled your heart.
You realize,
that the only time you truly have
is this one,
right here, right now.
And with that,
you live it with all your heart—
unapologetically, fully,
beautifully alive.

63. When the Soul Whispers

The soul never breaks all at once.
It unravels slowly, quietly—
through the tired sighs at the end of the day,
the heaviness in your chest,
the way simple joys start feeling out of reach.
At first, it's gentle.
A whisper. A soft nudge.
Slow down. Rest. Come back to yourself.
But you don't.
Life keeps pulling you forward,
and you tell yourself you'll rest later.
That it's just a phase.
That you're fine.
So, the whispers grow louder.
Sleep stops feeling restful.
The body aches in places it never did before.
You snap at the people you love,
feel distant from the things that once lit you up.
You keep going, but inside, something feels off.
The soul never wanted to fight you.

It never wanted to break you.
It just wanted you to listen.
To slow down before exhaustion forced you to.
To breathe before life became too heavy.
To give yourself the love and care you so freely give to
others.
So pause now.
Not when everything falls apart.
Not when you have no choice.
Now.
Because your soul is always speaking.
And if you don't listen to the whispers,
one day, they will turn into a scream.

64. Finding the Way Back

It doesn't happen in one big moment.
It happens in the quiet.
In the sigh you didn't mean to let out.
In the way your body feels heavier,
even when you've done nothing at all.
It's in the forced smile,
the *I'm fine* that doesn't feel true,
the way you keep moving
because stopping feels harder.
It's in the mornings that feel like a burden,
in the nights that don't bring rest,
in the way joy feels like something
that belongs to other people.
And then one day, in the middle of doing nothing
special,
it hits you—
I'm not okay.
And for a moment, you don't know what to do with it.
Because you've been holding it all together for so long.
Because people count on you.

Because you don't even remember how to fall apart.
But maybe, just maybe,
this is where healing begins.
Not in pretending.
Not in pushing through.
But in sitting with yourself,
holding your own heart gently,
and whispering, *It's okay to not be okay.*
And somehow, in that softness,
you start finding your way back.

65. Forgiving Yourself for What You Didn't Know

You didn't know then
what you know now.
You were doing your best
with the light you had,
even if now, that light feels dim.
You didn't know the right words,
the right choices,
the way things would unfold.
You were learning, stumbling,
figuring it out as you went.
And yet, you hold yourself to a standard
of someone who had already lived this life,
as if you should have known
how it would all turn out.
But love, how could you?
Growth is a path walked forward,
but understood in reverse.
Wisdom comes after the lesson,
not before.

So loosen your grip on regret.
Place your hand over your heart.
And whisper to the past versions of yourself
I forgive you.
For not knowing.
For not seeing.
For the choices you made with a tender heart,
even when they led you to pain.
You were never meant to get everything right.
You were only meant to grow.
And you have.
Oh, how you have.

66. A Letter to You

Dear You,

I want you to know—wherever you are in this moment, you are exactly where you need to be. Even if it doesn't feel like it. Even if the road ahead looks uncertain. Trust this: **you are not lost.** You are simply becoming.

Healing is not a race. There is no finish line, no perfect way to do it. Some days, you will feel strong and free. Other days, the past may whisper to you, and the weight of old wounds might feel heavy again. That's okay. Healing is not about never hurting again. It's about learning to hold yourself with love through it all. You are not behind. You are not broken. You are growing in ways you cannot yet see. Life is still unfolding for you, in ways that will one day make sense.

So take a deep breath. Trust the timing of your journey. Be patient with yourself. And remember, no matter what—**you are never alone, and you are always enough.**

With love,

Akanksha